MINDFUL HACKS FOR TEENS
WHEN LIFE FEELS OVERWHELMING

BY
H. J. RAY

MULTIRAY COPYRIGHT 2025. ALL RIGHTS RESERVED.

 BREAKING NEWS

===================

Life is weird, unpredictable, and occasionally a complete mess.

Some days you'll feel unstoppable. Other days, getting out of bed feels impossible. You'll overthink, procrastinate, spiral, doubt yourself, get annoyed at everything, and sometimes feel like an emotional train wreck for no clear reason.

THAT'S WHERE THIS BOOK COMES IN.

This isn't about "just think positive" or pretending emotions don't exist.

It's about learning how to work with your emotions, not against them.

HERE'S THE DEAL:

STEP 1:
✨ Emotions are signals. 📡

STEP 2:
🔢 You can hit pause & interrupt those signals. 🔀

STEP 3:
🔑 That pause = power. 🧠

🔥 THAT'S WHY THESE HACKS MATTER. THEY'RE POWERFUL SIGNAL-INTERRUPTERS. 🪨⚡

😠 » If you react straight from anger, you'll usually make things worse.

⏸ » If you pause, shift, and then respond… you step out of victim mode and into creator mode 🎨

🌀 The hacks help you break the cycle of emotions that keep you stuck.

🌊 The anchors help you ride your best states—creativity, flow, inspiration—and stay there longer.

⏳ Feelings pass. But your ability to shift your state and choose differently in the moment? 🔑

That's life-changing. 🌍💥

😠 VICTIM MODE

Emotions run the show
Blame others for how you feel
Let situations control your mood

"LIFE HAPPENS TO ME."

🎨 CREATOR MODE 🎨

Own your emotions
Choose your response
Shape your world from the inside out

"LIFE HAPPENS THROUGH ME."

IN THIS BOOK YOU'LL FIND 25 MINDFUL HACKS FOR SOS MOMENTS SPLIT INTO 5 ENERGY STATES:

LOW ENERGY
Exhausted, unmotivated, stuck.

MEDIUM ENERGY
Overthinking, stressed, second-guessing.

HIGH ENERGY
Anxious, frustrated, angry.

==

The threshold to Creator Mode — where you shape your world from the inside out.

==

PEAK STATES
Excited, inspired, creative.

EXPANSION STATES
Limitless & grounded.

HOW TO USE THIS BOOK

STEP 1:
🔍😌 Flip to the section that matches your current mood.

STEP 2:
📖 🧠 Read the hack, try the strategy.

STEP 3:
🔄⭐ Come back whenever you need a reset, reality check, or quick way to feel human again.

❗ This book won't fix everything. But it will help you handle life better.

So, ready?
Let's dive in. ⚡

CONTENTS

💤 LOW ENERGY
When getting up feels like a whole event.

⏰ SOS MOMENT: .... P. 14
"I can't get out of bed."

😔 SOS MOMENT: .... P. 16
"I feel like I'm not good enough."

😢 SOS MOMENT: .... P. 18
"I'm about to cry in a public place."

📱 SOS MOMENT: .... P. 20
"I'm scrolling instead of sleeping."

📅 SOS MOMENT: .... P. 22
"I'm a procrastination champion."

😣 MEDIUM ENERGY:
Second-guessing, regretting, and spiraling.

💡 **SOS MOMENT:** .... P. 26
"I'm feeling uninspired, but I don't know what to do about it."

😔 **SOS MOMENT:** .... P. 28
"I said yes to something I didn't want to do."

😟 **SOS MOMENT:** .... P. 30
"I'm regretting something I said or did."

😕 **SOS MOMENT:** .... P. 32
"I keep second-guessing myself."

🧩 **SOS MOMENT:** .... P. 34
"I'm stuck in a problem & don't know how to fix it."

✳ HIGH ENERGY:
You're wired, overstimulated, or on edge.

😟 SOS MOMENT: ....P. 38
"I'm worried about tomorrow."

😨 SOS MOMENT: ....P. 40
"I have a million things to do & I'm freaking out."

😵 SOS MOMENT: ....P. 42
"My anxiety is skyrocketing."

✳ SOS MOMENT: ....P. 44
"Everything is annoying me."

😡 SOS MOMENT: ....P. 46
"I'm so angry, I could flip a table."

⚡ PEAK STATES:
Those golden moments where life feels epic.

🎯 **SOS MOMENT:** ....P. 52
"I'm so hyper-focused, I forgot to eat."

💪 **SOS MOMENT:** ....P. 54
"I feel unstoppable—like I can take on the world."

🎨 **SOS MOMENT:** ....P. 56
"I just had the best idea ever—instant aha!"

😁 **SOS MOMENT:** ....P. 58
"I'm so hyped, I can't stop smiling."

🌊 **SOS MOMENT:** ....P. 60
"I feel completely in flow."

⭐ EXPANSION STATES
The "whoa" moments of complete clarity.

SOS MOMENT: .... P. 66
"I feel a deep acceptance of what is."

SOS MOMENT: .... P. 68
"I'm feeling so much love, I might explode."

SOS MOMENT: .... P. 70
"I'm at peace. for real."

SOS MOMENT: .... P. 72
"I feel enlightened. like, actual clarity."

SOS MOMENT: .... P. 74
"I feel completely outside my body—in a good way."

CHECKPOINT: BEFORE YOU DIVE IN

Ask yourself these three questions:

WHAT'S THE SIZE OF THIS FEELING?
(Is it small, medium, or so big it's hard to handle?)

AM I SAFE RIGHT NOW?
(Check your body, your environment, and your thoughts.)

DO I NEED EXTRA HELP?
(Sometimes talking to a friend, parent, or professional is the best next step.)

😩 LOW ENERGY 😩

(EXHAUSTED, UNMOTIVATED, STUCK)
WHEN GETTING UP FEELS LIKE
A WHOLE EVENT.

 SOS MOMENT

"I CAN'T GET OUT OF BED."

 BREAKING NEWS

========================

Scientists confirm that laying there overthinking will not, in fact, solve your problems.

✧ THE HACK ✧

STEP 1:
Put your feet against a wall. (Yes, really.) Shifts blood flow, refreshes your brain.

STEP 2:
Hit play on a pump-up track. (Instant vibe shift.)

STEP 3:
When the song ends, commit to one action: grab a glass of water, jump in the shower, or get dressed.

◎ WHY IT WORKS:
Your brain gets stuck in freeze mode, but small shifts = big mental resets.

 SOS MOMENT

"I FEEL LIKE I'M NOT GOOD ENOUGH."

 BREAKING NEWS

======================

The people you admire also have no idea what they're doing.

✨ THE HACK ✨

STEP 1:
Catch It.
Notice the thought and say (in your head or out loud): "I caught you." Place one hand over your chest. This signals safety to your body.

STEP 2:
With your other hand, gently tap your temple three times while saying: "I am enough." Add a steady breath in through your nose, out through your mouth with each tap.

STEP 3:
Stand up tall. Roll your shoulders back. Take one deep breath and stretch your arms wide like you're taking up space.
Say: "I belong here."

🎯 WHY IT WORKS:
Touching your temples interrupts looping negative thoughts and anchors you in the present moment.

😭 SOS MOMENT 😭

"I'M ABOUT TO CRY IN A PUBLIC PLACE."

🚨 BREAKING NEWS 🚨

========================

Holding back tears does not make you stronger.
It just gives you a headache.

✦ THE HACK ✦
WHEN YOU NEED TO HOLD IT TOGETHER (FOR NOW)

STEP 1:

Gently press your tongue to the roof of your mouth. This tells your body to pause the tear reflex.

STEP 2:

Roll your shoulders back, then lightly squeeze one shoulder with your opposite hand. Switch sides. It grounds you fast.

STEP 3:

Breathe in through your nose, out slowly through pursed lips like you're blowing through a straw. Instant calm.

◎ WHY IT WORKS:

Jaw, shoulders, and breath all send "I'm safe" messages to your nervous system, short-circuiting the overwhelm before tears spill.

📱 SOS MOMENT 📱
"I'M SCROLLING INSTEAD OF SLEEPING."

======================

Tomorrow will thank you if you log off now.

✦ THE HACK ✦

STEP 1:
Turn your screen to grayscale. Your brain finds black-and-white incredibly boring.

STEP 2:
Tense every muscle in your body—squeeze from head to toe.

STEP 3:
Release into your bed and pillow like melting butter. With each breath, let go a little more - don't stop until you drift into sleep.

◎ WHY IT WORKS:
Body shift from wired to tired.

📅 SOS MOMENT 📅
"I'M A PROCRASTINATION CHAMPION."

🚨 BREAKING NEWS 🚨
========================
Studies show: The hardest part of doing something is... starting.

✦ THE HACK ✦

STEP 1:
Write your task down on paper.
(Get it out of your head.)

STEP 2:
Split it into the tiniest parts possible. (E.g., "Open laptop," "Write subject line.")

STEP 3:
Do just one. Tick it off. Feel the dopamine. Repeat if you want—momentum is sneaky like that.

🎯 WHY IT WORKS:
Your brain loves finishing things. Checking off even a micro-task gives a reward hit that fuels the next step. Tiny wins snowball into movement.

CHECKPOINT: BEFORE YOU DIVE IN

Ask yourself these three questions:

WHAT'S THE SIZE OF THIS FEELING?
(Is it small, medium, or so big it's hard to handle?)

AM I SAFE RIGHT NOW?
(Check your body, your environment, and your thoughts.)

DO I NEED EXTRA HELP?
(Sometimes talking to a friend, parent, or professional is the best next step.)

😐 MEDIUM ENERGY
SECOND-GUESSING · REGRETTING · SPIRALING

💡 SOS MOMENT 💡
"I'M FEELING UNINSPIRED, BUT I DON'T KNOW WHAT TO DO ABOUT IT."

 BREAKING NEWS

=======================

Studies show: Creativity hates routine.

✦ THE HACK ✦

STEP 1:
Go on a micro-adventure. Step outside, walk a new path.

STEP 2:
Notice things like you're seeing them for the first time.

STEP 3:
Remember: you can't force creativity. (It's like trying to tickle yourself—doesn't work.) Let your brain relax and the flow sneaks back in.

◎ WHY IT WORKS:
Fresh air + novelty reset your perspective. When you stop chasing ideas, your brain finally has room to deliver them.

SOS MOMENT

"I SAID YES TO SOMETHING I DIDN'T WANT TO DO."

 BREAKING NEWS

========================

A past "yes" is not a lifetime contract. You're allowed to change your mind.

THE HACK

STEP 1:

Breathe in as deeply as you can. Exhale in three sharp, strong breaths. Repeat three times.

STEP 2:

Stand with your feet hip-width apart, knees soft. Push your hands out in front of you (palms facing outward, like a stop sign). Hold for three seconds, then bring your hands back to your chest and rest them there.

STEP 3:

Practice this line: "I changed my mind." No excuses, no people-pleasing.

🎯 WHY IT WORKS:
- Exhales release stress that fuels people-pleasing.
- Stop-palms signal "no," anchoring safety and self-protection.
- Hands to chest remind you that your needs matter too.

SOS MOMENT
"I'M REGRETTING SOMETHING I SAID OR DID."

🚨 BREAKING NEWS 🚨
========================
Replaying the situation 500 times does not change the outcome.

✦ THE HACK ✦

STEP 1:
Close your eyes. Breathe deeply. Visualize the moment playing out the way you wish it had gone. See and feel yourself handling it with confidence and care.

STEP 2:
If it needs fixing, say: "Hey, I was thinking about that moment, and I just wanted to clarify…"

STEP 3:
Write down the lesson. Then crumple or rip the paper — a physical signal that you're moving on.

◎ WHY IT WORKS:
- Visualisation rewires your brain with a new "preferred" memory, so you're ready next time.
- Physical release (speaking, writing, or ripping) closes the loop so your body knows it's done.

😕 SOS MOMENT 😕
"I KEEP SECOND-GUESSING MYSELF."

===================

Overthinking doesn't give you new answers —it just puts the same ones on repeat.

✦ THE HACK ✦

STEP 1:
Flip a coin—not to decide, but to test your gut. Notice if you're secretly relieved or disappointed by the result.

STEP 2:
Write down the best-case scenario—the way you want it to work out. Clarity looks better on paper.

STEP 3:
Take a deep breath, make your choice, and line up with it. Trust that with the info you had, you made the best call you could. From here on, only look forward.

◎ WHY IT WORKS:
Second-guessing fades when you shift from fear of being wrong to confidence in moving forward.

🧩 SOS MOMENT 🧩

"I'M STUCK IN A PROBLEM AND DON'T KNOW HOW TO FIX IT."

 **BREAKING NEWS** 🚨

========================

Your brain believes whatever script you feed it. Change the script, change the outcome.

THE HACK

STEP 1:

Catch your words.
Saying "I don't know how" or "I can't figure this out" tells your brain to give up. It locks onto the problem instead of finding solutions.

STEP 2:

Try: "How will I figure this out?" or "I haven't figured it out yet." Even "I don't know how... for now." These phrases turn your brain into a solution-hunter instead of a problem-repeater.

STEP 3:

Quit obsessing. Go for a walk, play a game, listen to music. The answer usually shows up when your brain is relaxed, not when it's spiralling.

◎ WHY IT WORKS:

Language directs focus. Relaxation unlocks the creative mode where breakthroughs live.

CHECKPOINT: BEFORE YOU DIVE IN

Ask yourself these three questions:

WHAT'S THE SIZE OF THIS FEELING?
(Is it small, medium, or so big it's hard to handle?)

AM I SAFE RIGHT NOW?
(Check your body, your environment, and your thoughts.)

DO I NEED EXTRA HELP?
(Sometimes talking to a friend, parent, or professional is the best next step.)

HIGH ENERGY

ANXIOUS · FRUSTRATED · ANGRY
WHEN YOU FEEL LIKE LAUNCHING
YOURSELF INTO SPACE.

😟 **SOS MOMENT** 😟
"I'M WORRIED ABOUT TOMORROW."

 **BREAKING NEWS**

======================

The future isn't here yet—stop rehearsing disasters.

✦ THE HACK ✦

STEP 1:
Close your eyes and picture it playing out exactly how you want. See it, feel it, own it.

STEP 2:
Release the urge to control every detail. Trust the process—you've set the scene.

STEP 3:
IN THE MORNING: Hit play on your feel-good soundtrack and ride the day like a pro.

◎ WHY IT WORKS:
Visualisation primes your brain to expect success. Letting go reduces anxiety. Music boosts mood + energy so you meet the day on your terms.

🐨 SOS MOMENT 🐨
"I HAVE A MILLION THINGS TO DO AND I'M FREAKING OUT."

======================
Panicking is not a productivity tool.

✦ THE HACK ✦

STEP 1:

Close your eyes and move your awareness to the back of your skull. Feel the space there. This instantly pulls you out of "front-brain panic mode."

STEP 2:

Imagine standing under a shower. Let all the stress and noise rinse off your head and body, swirling down the drain. (Splash cool water on your face if you can.)

STEP 3:

Write everything down. Circle the one most important thing and do that first.

🎯 WHY IT WORKS:

- Back-of-skull focus stops your brain from spinning out.
- Shower vibe = instant reset, like hitting refresh.

SOS MOMENT
"MY ANXIETY IS SKYROCKETING."

 BREAKING NEWS

======================

You are NOT your anxiety.

✦ THE HACK ✦

STEP 1:
Shake your hands like you're flinging off something sticky. Let your arms loosen and drop the tension.

STEP 2:
Name 5 things you see, 4 you can touch, 3 you hear, 2 you smell, 1 you taste. Bring your senses back to right now.

STEP 3:
Say to yourself: "This will pass." Because it always does.

🎯 WHY IT WORKS:
- Shaking dumps nervous energy and adrenaline.
- 5-4-3-2-1 snaps your brain out of the future and back into the present.
- Mantra reminds you anxiety is temporary, not forever.

SOS MOMENT
"EVERYTHING IS ANNOYING ME."

==================

Experts confirm: It's probably not everyone else. It's definitely your nervous system in fight mode.

✦ THE HACK ✦

STEP 1:
Notice & Celebrate.
The fact you caught it before snapping is a win. Take one breath in and nod to yourself: "I see it."

STEP 2:
Press the tip of each finger to your thumb, one at a time. Focus on the sensation as you cycle through. This shifts your attention off the trigger.

STEP 3:
Blow out a slow sigh or shake out your arms. Let the leftover frustration exit your body.

◎ WHY IT WORKS:
- Noticing early stops anger from hijacking you.
- Finger pressing calms the nervous system by giving your brain a new focus.
- Gentle release clears out the tension before it builds into snapping.

😠 SOS MOMENT 😠

"I'M SO ANGRY, I COULD FLIP A TABLE."

🚨 BREAKING NEWS 🚨

========================

Studies show: Flipping actual tables is frowned upon.

✦ THE HACK ✦

STEP 1:
Burn It (if you can).
If you can step away, do something physical: run, 10 push-ups, sprint stairs, or scream into a pillow. Get the energy out fast.

STEP 2:
Hold It (if you can't).
If you're stuck in public, take the slowest breath possible in through your nose, then release it through pursed lips. While breathing, scrunch your toes hard, then release them into the floor.

STEP 3:
Choose Your Energy.
Ask yourself: "Is this really worth my energy?" If yes, respond with calm strength. If no, let it go and save your power.

◎ WHY IT WORKS:
- Physical release burns off fight-mode energy.
- Slow breath + toes calm your body when you can't move.
- Energy check gives you back control: you decide where your fire goes.

CHECKPOINT: BEFORE YOU DIVE IN

Ask yourself these three questions:

WHAT'S THE SIZE OF THIS FEELING?
(Am I buzzing, bursting, or riding a steady high?)

AM I STILL CARING FOR MY BODY?
(Food, water, rest—even peak energy needs balance.)

HOW CAN I USE THIS ENERGY WELL?
(Channel it into something creative, fun, or meaningful.)

😎 PEAK STATES 😎

EXCITEMENT, JOY, HYPE, INSPIRATION
(BIG, BRIGHT, SHORT-LIVED)
THRESHOLD TO CREATOR MODE.

Good vibes aren't forever, but they're forever yours. Save the memory, lock in the feeling, and hit replay whenever you need it.

⚡ PEAK STATES: THE GOOD STUFF

🎇 WARNING: These states are not permanent. And that's okay.

Happiness, love, excitement, inspiration, connection—all of them come and go. The trick isn't to grip them too tightly but to ride the wave while it's here and use anchors to come back when they drift.

When you find yourself in one of these peak states, soak it in. Roll around in it. Memorize it. Because this is the good stuff.

These hacks aren't about making these feelings last forever. That's not how emotions work. Instead, these are anchors—ways to return to these states when you need them.

🎯 PEAK STATE 🎯

"I'M SO HYPER-FOCUSED, I FORGOT TO EAT."

 BREAKING NEWS

====================

You are a productivity machine.

THE ANCHOR

STEP 1:
Notice what got you here: the music, the vibe, the setup.

STEP 2:
Without breaking focus, soften your gaze. Sense your peripheral vision—that's everything you can see out of the corners of your eyes. Expand your awareness beyond what's directly in front of you and take in the whole picture.

STEP 3:
Set a timer for breaks—water, food, stretch. Flow naturally rises and fades, and caring for your body keeps it coming back stronger.

🎯 WHY IT WORKS:
- Music + vibe = repeatable recipe for focus.
- Peripheral vision = relaxes the mind while sharpening awareness.
- Breaks = protect your energy so the zone returns naturally.

PEAK STATE

"I FEEL UNSTOPPABLE — LIKE I CAN TAKE ON THE WORLD."

 BREAKING NEWS

========================

Experts agree: This is what main character energy actually feels like.

THE ANCHOR

STEP 1:
Breathe it deep. Notice the air, the space, the aliveness around you. Let it charge you up.

STEP 2:
Pick one thing to hold this feeling—a rock, a word, a song, even a scent. That's your touchstone.

STEP 3:
Get to a mirror. Look yourself in the eyes, tilt your chin up, puff your chest out, give yourself a wink: "Yes you— you epic human."

◎ WHY IT WORKS:
- Breathing it in locks the vibe in deeper.
- Anchors (like a song or object) make it easy to get the feeling back.
- Mirror power hard-wires confidence straight into you.

🎨 PEAK STATE 🎨
"I just had the best idea ever- instant aha!"

🚨 BREAKING NEWS 🚨
======================

Studies Show: Inspiration is a guest that leaves when ignored.

THE ANCHOR

STEP 1:

Capture it immediately. Voice note, scribble, whatever—don't assume you'll remember later.

STEP 2:

Move while inspired. Go for a walk, dance, stretch—physical movement keeps the ideas flowing.

STEP 3:

Avoid perfection traps. Don't worry about "good," just get it down.

◎ WHY IT WORKS:

Inspiration moves fast. If you honor it when it arrives, it visits more often.

😁 **PEAK STATE** 😁

"I'M SO HYPED, I CAN'T STOP SMILING."

🚨 **BREAKING NEWS** 🚨

Fact check: It takes more muscles to frown than to smile.

✦ THE ANCHOR ✦

STEP 1:
Feel It.
As you smile, imagine it glowing through your whole body—heart, chest, down your arms, into your hands. Let it charge you up.

STEP 2:
Amplify It.
Pick a song that matches your mood and crank it up. Let the music expand the hype and lock it in as your anchor.

STEP 3:
Use It.
This is prime energy. Put it into action—start the thing, share the joy, move with it.

🎯 WHY IT WORKS:

- Smiling through your body infuses every cell with energy.
- Music boosts the vibe and gives you a replay button for joy.
- Taking action turns hype into momentum that lasts.

🌙 PEAK STATE 🌙
"I FEEL COMPLETELY IN FLOW."

🚨 BREAKING NEWS 🚨
======================
Scientists confirm: This is the state athletes, artists, and monks chase daily.

THE ANCHOR

STEP 1:
Sense the soles of your feet on the ground and the steady beat of your heart. Feel the connection between your body and emotions.

STEP 2:
Now lift your awareness to the crown of your head. Breathe into the link between body, heart, and mind. This alignment is flow—this is where magic happens and you become unstoppable.

STEP 3:
Don't overthink it. Flow fades when you analyse it. Just keep moving inside the moment.

WHY IT WORKS:
- Grounding in feet + heart roots you in your body and emotions.
- Aligning with your head connects mind and body, deepening flow.
- Presence keeps you surfing the wave without breaking it.

CHECKPOINT: BEFORE YOU DIVE IN

Ask yourself these three questions:

WHAT'S THE SIZE OF THIS AWARENESS?
(Is it a gentle calm or a huge sense of connection?)

AM I GROUNDED IN MY BODY?
(Can I feel my feet, breath, or heart while expanding?)

HOW CAN I RETURN HERE AGAIN?
(Notice the anchor—heart, spine, vision—so you can revisit this state.)

😇 EXPANSION STATES 😇
ALIGNMENT, LOVE, STEADY, LIMITLESS & GROUNDED.

Expansion states are like shooting stars—brief, brilliant, and unforgettable. Let them light you up and guide your steps.

⭐ EXPANDING INTO AWARENESS

🔅 FINAL WARNING: These states are not everyday experiences. They come in waves—let them arrive, let them go, and trust that they will return.

Sometimes, you get a glimpse beyond the noise—a deep sense of acceptance, self-awareness, or even an out-of-body perspective.

These moments change you.

These aren't hacks to control the feeling. They're anchors to honour it when it arrives.

🌀 EXPANSION STATE 🌀
"I FEEL A DEEP ACCEPTANCE OF WHAT IS."

🚨 BREAKING NEWS 💥

========================

Scientists confirm: Surrender is not giving up—it's finding peace with what is.

✦ THE ANCHOR ✦

STEP 1:
Close your eyes. Place a hand on your chest. Breathe slowly into your heart space, as if your breath moves in and out from there.

STEP 2:
Notice where relief shows up—maybe in your shoulders dropping, your jaw softening, or your belly loosening. Let your body teach you what acceptance feels like.

STEP 3:
Release the urge to hold onto this state. Acceptance isn't about clutching—it's about gently returning here again and again.

◎ WHY IT WORKS:
- Heart breathing makes acceptance something you feel, not just think.
- Body scan shows you where calm lives in your body.
- Softening reminds you this isn't a one-time thing—you can always come back.

🧡 **EXPANSION STATE** 🧡

"I'M FEELING SO MUCH LOVE, I MIGHT EXPLODE."

###

`=====================`

Scientists confirm this feeling is real and should be fully embraced.

THE ANCHOR

STEP 1:
Notice where the love shows up in your body—maybe a warm chest, a buzzing face, or butterflies in your stomach. Memorise it.

STEP 2:
Say it out loud: "I love this moment," "I love you," or even just "Wow." Words amplify the feeling."

STEP 3:
Grab your journal and capture the moment. Write what you're grateful for right now. The more you lean into it, the more love grows.

⊚ WHY IT WORKS:
- Feeling it in your body makes love a real, physical state.
- Speaking it out loud strengthens the emotion.
- Writing it down locks it in your memory and gives you a way to return to it later.

EXPANSION STATE
"I'M AT PEACE. FOR REAL."

========================
You are allowed to feel good without guilt.

THE ANCHOR

STEP 1:
Close your eyes. Run your awareness down your spine. Feel each muscle relax as you anchor into this moment.

STEP 2:
With every inhale, feel peace spreading through your body—sinking into your bones, filling every part of you.

STEP 3:
Don't grab at the peace. Holding on too tightly creates tension. Just let it move through you naturally.

◎ WHY IT WORKS:
- Spine awareness grounds peace in your body.
- Breathing it deeper infuses calm into every cell.
- Letting it be keeps peace natural instead of forced.

🧘 EXPANSION STATE 🧘
"I FEEL ENLIGHTENED. LIKE, ACTUAL CLARITY."

💥 BREAKING NEWS 💥
========================

Studies show: You may or may not be a monk now.

THE ANCHOR

STEP 1:

Place your palms together and lightly connect your fingertips, as if holding a soft ball between your hands.

STEP 2:

Close your eyes and imagine a bright ball of light glowing in that space. With each breath, let the light grow stronger.

STEP 3:

Spread that light through your whole body—into your chest, your arms, your legs, all the way to your fingertips and toes. Let the feeling of clarity fill every cell.

◎ WHY IT WORKS:

- The fingertip connection creates a physical anchor for focus.
- Visualising light taps into the mind-body link and makes clarity feel real.
- Expanding it through the body imprints the state, so you can return to it whenever you need.

🌌 EXPANSION STATE 🌌
"I FEEL COMPLETELY OUTSIDE MY BODY —IN A GOOD WAY."

🚨 BREAKING NEWS 🚨
===================
Studies show: This is what monks, astronauts, and artists chase.

THE ANCHOR

STEP 1:

Close your eyes and feel the entire surface of your body—skin, clothes, air touching you. Then sink deeper into that awareness.

STEP 2:

Now imagine lifting above yourself, seeing your body from the outside. Notice how you're connected to everything around you.

STEP 3:

Anchor the feeling by sensing your feet and imagining roots growing deep into the earth. Feel stable, grounded, and connected.

◎ WHY IT WORKS:

- Sensing your body grounds you before expanding.
- Helicopter view gives perspective and connection beyond yourself.
- Rooting back in makes the expansion safe, steady, and repeatable.

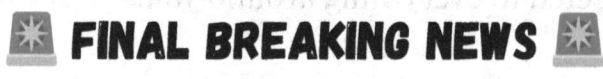

========================
You are not your bad days.

No matter how chaotic or messy life gets, you're not broken.

Emotions aren't problems to fix—they're signals you can list to, interrupt and retune.

WHEN IN DOUBT, REMEMBER:

✓ You always have a choice. Even if it's just choosing to take one deep breath.

Life will keep life-ing.

FINAL THINGS TO REMEMBER:

✓ No emotion lasts forever. Ride the wave. It always shifts.
✓ You are not your thoughts. Just because your brain says it doesn't mean it's true.
✓ You don't have to do this perfectly. Just try. That's enough.

Some days, you'll need these hacks. Other days, you won't. Either way? You've got this.

BONUS POWER HABIT
"I THINK I'M ACTUALLY OKAY."

🚨 BREAKING NEWS 🚨
========================
Look at you, thriving.

Mindful hacks are awesome in the moment—when you're spiraling, stressing, or just need to feel human again. But here's the secret: the best way to deal with SOS moments is to set yourself up before they even show up.

High performers, athletes, and creators don't just wing it. They prime their day. Translation: they wake up and decide how they want to feel, then do something small to lock it in.

SOME SIMPLE WAYS TO PRIME YOUR DAY:

- Intention setting – pick the vibe you want (calm, focused, confident) before the world decides it for you.

- Move your body – stretch, do a workout, or just blast music and dance around your room.

- Meditation or journaling – clear your mind or dump your thoughts so they don't clutter your whole day.

Here's the deal: you can stack money, followers, and shiny stuff all day—but if your head's a mess and your emotions run the show, you won't enjoy a second of it.

THE REAL FLEX? YOUR INNER GAME.

Care less about the noise. Run your own race. Feel good for the sake of feeling good. That's when your brain works smarter, your ideas take off, and you literally train yourself for the life you want from the inside-out.

That's the power of priming your day.

⚡ 21-DAY MORNING PRIME CHALLENGE ⚡

(before you touch your phone)

WRITE (1 MIN)
Journal one line: "Today I choose ___." What state do you want to be in?

BREATHE (2 MIN)
Anchor it with five slow, deep breaths.

MOVE (2 MIN)
Push-ups, sit-ups, squats, or just wiggle & shake.

✅ TICK. BREATHE. 🔄 REPEAT.

Can you challenge yourself for 21 days?

Watch your focus sharpen, your mood lift, and your resilience build—so when SOS moments hit, they land softer and you bounce back faster.

DAILY TRACKER

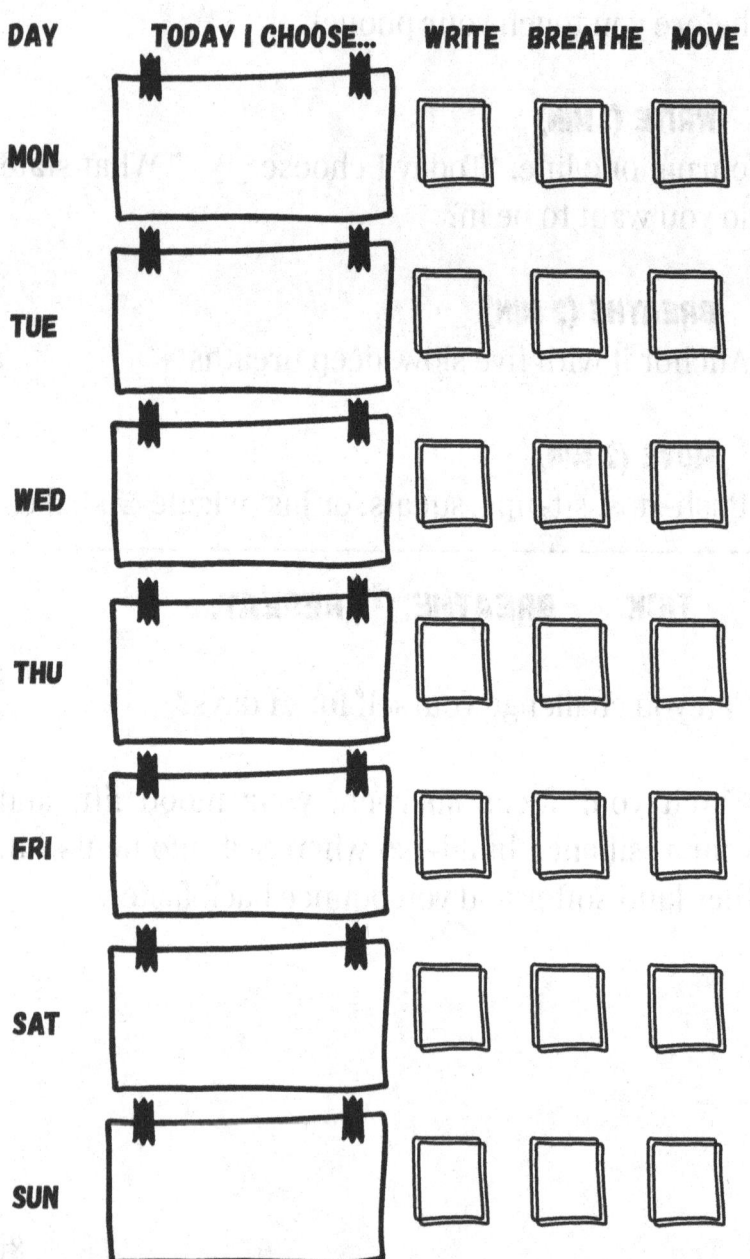

WEEKLY REFLECTION

- Did I have an SOS moment? Which hack did I use?

- Did I experience a Peak State? How did I anchor it in?

- How am I feeling compared to Day 1?

- One thing I noticed about myself:

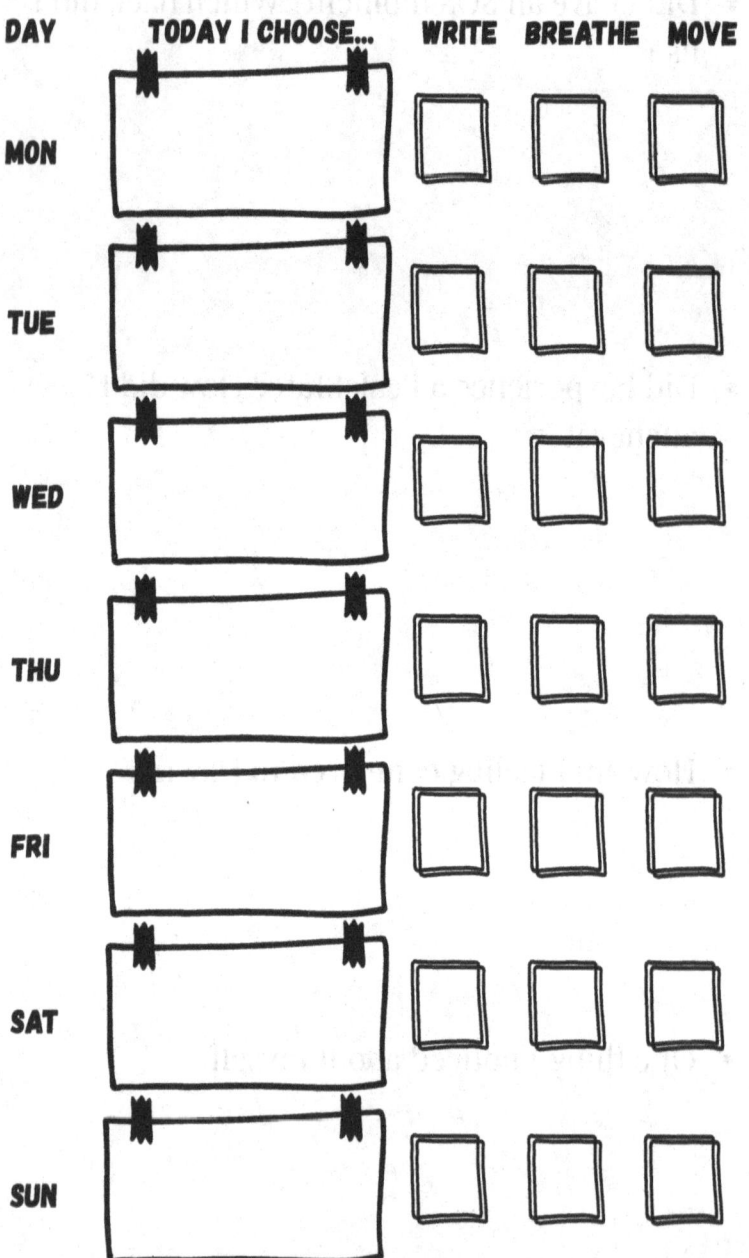

WEEKLY REFLECTION

- Did I have an SOS moment? Which hack did I use?

- Did I experience a Peak State? How did I anchor it in?

- How am I feeling compared to Day 1?

- One thing I noticed about myself:

DAILY TRACKER

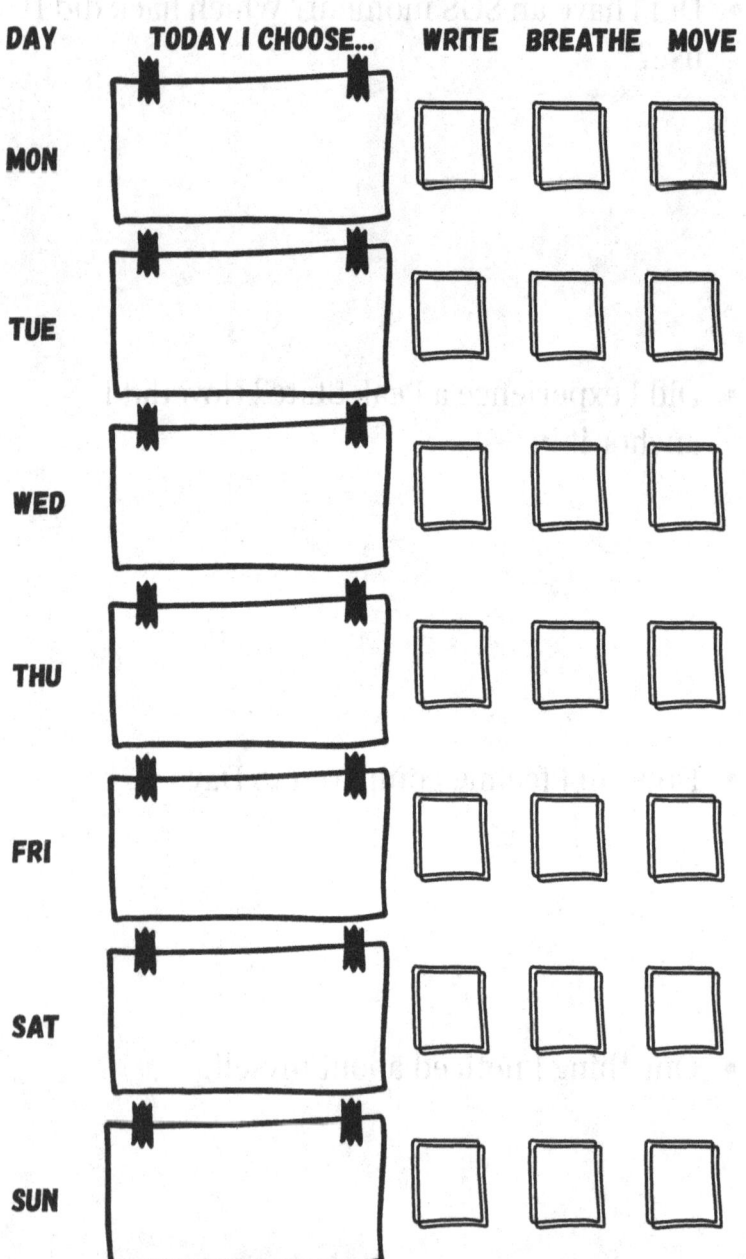

WEEKLY REFLECTION

- Did I have an SOS moment? Which hack did I use?

- Did I experience a Peak State? How did I anchor it in?

- How am I feeling compared to Day 1?

- One thing I noticed about myself:

NOTES TO SELF:

- Did I give an SOS moment? Which hack did I use?

- Did I reinforce a limit, a Pivot Stage, Boundary, and/or option to opt out?

- What kind of behavior did I see?

- Who did or did not debate myself?

MULTIRAY is an internationally recognised provider of resources that support emotional literacy, resilience-building, and mental health. Its playful, practical tools, created by founder Heather Ray, are trusted by families, schools, and therapists worldwide.

The school partners with Liverpool John Moores University, whose research underpins and validates the outcomes of its programs, and with Good Shepherd ANZ, whose courageous and compassionate service extends their reach across communities. Together, these collaborations ensure the work is innovative, evidence-based, and grounded in real-world impact.

THIS ISN'T THE END—JUST THE BEGINNING!
Discover more books, hacks, and resources at:
www.multiray.com.au

P.S. You are amazing.

www.ingramcontent.com/pod-product-compliance
Lightning Source LLC
Chambersburg PA
CBHW011151290426
44109CB00025B/2572